SO-BAP-480

THE LIONFISH COOKBOOK

The Caribbean's New Delicacy

by
Reef Environmental
Education Foundation

REEF
www.REEF.org

Photo by Rich Carey

RECIPES AND TEXT
TRICIA FERGUSON
AND
LAD AKINS

RECIPE PHOTOGRAPHY
DAVID M. STONE

Copyright © 2010 Reef Environmental Education Foundation

All Rights Reserved. No part of this book may be reproduced in part or in whole or transmitted in any form or by any means, electronic, mechanical, photocopying, recording, or otherwise, without prior written permission of REEF, with the exception of reviewers, who may quote brief quotations in connection with a review in a newspaper, magazine, or electronic publication.

Recipe photography by David M. Stone
Cover and cookbook design by Joanne Kidd, Jacksonville, FL

Published by:
Reef Environmental Education Foundation (REEF)
98300 Overseas Highway, Key Largo, FL 33037
(305) 852-0030 | www.REEF.org

Printed in the United States of America

ISBN: 978-0-615-42892-5

Proceeds to benefit REEF and marine conservation.

Contents

Contents

Seven Stars – The Luxury Resort on Grace Bay, Turks and Caicos

ACKNOWLEDGEMENTS

The proceeds from the sale of this book will continue to support marine conservation, lionfish research and control programs as long as there are oceans.

This book is the result of ongoing efforts throughout the Caribbean and US to address the rapid invasion of the Indo-Pacific lionfish. Listing everyone who has in some way influenced its creation would take a volume in itself.

The Lionfish Cookbook had its genesis in discussions with James Morris at NOAA, and his valued input in all things lionfish have been a great source of insight and encouragement. Continued collaboration and partnership with Stephanie Green at Simon Fraser University provided valuable input into all aspects of this book. Dive operators Bruce Purdy, Stuart Cove, Peter Hughes, and Alan and Clare Jardine provided logistical support for lionfish research and collections. The National Aquarium and Bermuda Aquarium assisted in collecting efforts and program development.

The dishes in this book and accompanying images were prepared at the prestigious Seven Stars Resort on Provodenciales in the Turks and Caicos Islands. Great thanks to this beautiful property for opening up their entire kitchen and facilitating this work, and to David Stone and family for their incredible hospitality and support. Joanne Kidd provided excellent edits, design, and layout of the book. Thanks to the contributions and active support of the entire REEF membership whose efforts in marine conservation are a shining example of grassroots success. Finally, thanks to David Ferguson, Robert and Linda Griffin, and Joe and Terri Manchisi in Eleuthera for being patient and gracious testers and helping to refine the recipes. The proceeds from the sale of this book support marine conservation, lionfish research and control programs.

Photo courtesy of Lad Akins / REEF

INTRODUCTION

This book provides a unique blend of tantalizing recipes, background on the invasion and its impacts, and information on how to safely catch, handle and prepare the fish.

Why a Lionfish Cookbook?

In their native range, Indo-Pacific lionfish are an uncommon and beautiful sight, with their populations in balance with the rest of nature. However, man has introduced lionfish to North America via the aquarium trade and his subsequent carelessness has resulted in invasive populations that are harming the marine ecosystems and economies of coastal North, Central and South America, the Caribbean, Bahamas, and Gulf of Mexico. Lionfish are the most recent man-made problem to threaten marine life across the region. But, as with all things, problems create opportunities for creative solutions and, in this case, the solution has a culinary twist. Lionfish are a tasty intruder with moist, buttery meat that is sure to make your mouth water.

While it is highly unlikely that lionfish will ever be eradicated from their invaded range, it is very possible that their populations can be controlled and their impacts minimized simply by adding them to the menu. While many traditional native seafood species are under immense fishing pressure and in need of protection, lionfish are a tasty, nutritious and environmentally conscious seafood choice. There is simply no "greener" fish to eat!

So whether you are reading this book to learn more about the lionfish invasion, create one of the scrumptious recipes, or support the concept of eating our way out of a tight spot, we applaud your choice and encourage you to, as Bermuda so aptly coined, "Eat 'em to Beat 'em!"

Eat 'em to Beat 'em!

REEF Volunteers Returning from a Lionfish Research Dive in the Bahamas

About REEF

The Reef Environmental Education Foundation is a non-profit marine conservation organization founded in 1990 to engage volunteers in the preservation of our marine systems.

From meager beginnings, the organization has grown to over 40,000 members engaged in highly effective and innovative conservation programs including the Fish Survey Project, the Great Annual Fish Count, the Grouper Moon spawning aggregation project, Artificial Reef studies and the Exotic Species program. The projects and programs coordinated by REEF's staff engage local communities and visitors in active, hands-on conservation. Operating as a small organization has its challenges, however, it also enables the organization to move quickly in addressing emerging issues. As such, REEF is often at the forefront of marine conservation issues and their solutions.

Relative to the invasive lionfish issue, REEF has been leading efforts around the region including cutting edge research, outreach and education, training in collecting and handling techniques, development of regional strategies, and organizing effective removal programs such as derbies and volunteer control teams. None of this work would be possible without the strong partnerships and collaborative efforts with key organizations and institutions. Foremost in these partnerships are those with the National Oceanic and Atmospheric Administration (NOAA), Simon Fraser University (SFU), and the United States Geologic Survey (USGS) who have crossed agency and international boundaries to better understand and address the invasion. REEF members highlight the concern and high regard for conservation of ocean systems held by peoples throughout the world. It is this regard for our oceans and marine life that drive effective programs and allow innovative projects, like this cookbook, to move forward into conservation reality. For those wishing to join in these efforts, REEF membership is free and the benefits ample. Learn more about REEF and become a member by visiting our website at www.REEF.org. Please feel free to contact REEF anytime for more information.

REEF
www.REEF.org

The first ever cookbook for an invasive marine fish

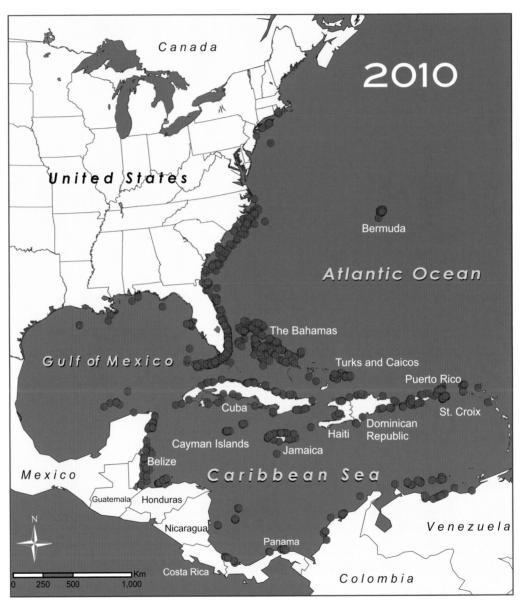

Current distribution of lionfish invasion as of September 2010. Courtesy of USGS

THE INVASIVE LIONFISH

(Pterois volitans, Pterois miles)

Background of the Invasion

For fishwatchers, aquarists, photographers and those who appreciate beauty in nature, lionfish are among the most dramatic and interesting of the tropical marine fishes. Native to a vast region of the Indo-Pacific and the Red Sea, the fish are members of the broadly diverse scorpionfish family, so named for their venomous spines. Most members of this group are somewhat drab in coloration and sedentary in their behavior, choosing to ambush prey rather than expend energy hunting. Lionfish are however, an exception. Their boldly patterned bodies, ornate fins and active predation make them a favorite among fish enthusiasts. In fact, their popularity as aquarium fish has led to the exportation of lionfish from the native range by the tens of thosands each year into markets around the world. Of course lionfish are not the only fish collected and traded in the aquarium industry, but are among the most ideally positioned to cause trouble – a near perfect invader.

Intentionally or not, lionfish have been introduced into South Florida waters. With a large human population in close proximity to coastal waters, south Florida is a hotbed of non-native sightings – with over 30 different species of non-native marine fish confirmed. Almost all of these cases have consisted of single or few isolated reports that did not persist over time, except for lionfish. With Florida records dating back as far as 1985, lionfish have more recently become established and are spreading throughout the region. Lionfish represent the first successful marine fish invasion in the Western Atlantic, and are expanding their range and increasing in numbers at a rate and magnitude never seen before.

There is simply no "greener" fish to eat.

Lionfish Biology, Ecology & Impacts

The same characteristics that make lionfish challenging to keep in home aquariums (rapid growth, voracious feeding and venomous spines) are likely the key characteristics that have allowed them to become such a successful invader. With growth rates of up to 7 inches per year lionfish are capable of growing faster than similar-sized native species with which they compete (small groupers and snappers). While growth and size at reproductive maturity varies among individual fish, on average, female lionfish can reproduce at about 5.5 inches and males at a tiny 3.5 inches, this means that lionfish less than a year old are already contributing to the next generation.

Lionfish spawn in pairs, the male and female exhibit extensive courtship leading up to a late night spawning event. During spawning, the female releases two buoyant masses of eggs that are fertilized by the male on their way to the surface. The eggs are surrounded by a mucous-like mass containing a chemical deterrent to predation. After drifting on the surface for a few days, the egg masses begin to break apart and the fertilized eggs hatch into what is referred to as larval stage fish. These mostly clear lionfish larvae drift in the currents for about a month, during which time they rapidly mature into juvenile fish before settling to the bottom. Once on the bottom, lionfish begin to exhibit their characteristic dark and light coloration, and continue to grow rapidly, consuming prey at alarming rates.

Studies in the lab and on the reefs have shown that lionfish are generalist predators capable of consuming prey up to half their own body size, with a stomach that can expand up to 30 times its empty size. Lionfish diets are very broad and include both fish and crustaceans. Stomach content studies have documented well over 50 species of prey including commercially, recreationally and ecologically important species. Juvenile grouper, snapper and parrotfish, as well as cleaner species like hogfish and wrasses, are regularly found in lionfish stomachs. The environmental effects of this predation are likely to be widespread, as these prey represent key elements of the marine systems. Groupers and snappers represent top predators and are economically important as highly regarded seafood. Parrot-fish are grazers and play key roles in keeping excess algae growth in check, preventing overgrowth of corals and maintaining healthy relationships on the reef. Cleaner species such as banded coral shrimp and bluehead wrasse maintain the health of other fish, acting as dentists and doctors by removing parasites and cleaning wounded areas of dead flesh. All of these species and more are being consumed at unsustainable rates. Without lionfish population controls, native species populations are likely to decrease dramatically, with some commercial species reduced to unharvestable levels and the possibility of extinction of vulnerable reef species.

Photo courtesy of Curtis W. Callaway

What about lionfish as prey? In witnessing the speed and intensity of this invasion, it certainly appears that few if any native predators are able to control lionfish populations. A few sporadic cases have been documented of grouper, eels or sharks consuming lionfish that are offered up, but virtually no predation on live lionfish has been observed. Of course, why would any predator choose prey with a formidable array of venomous spines?

Venom

Even in their larval stage lionfish are equipped with venomous spines. Their 13 dorsal spines, 2 pelvic spines and 3 anal spines contain grooves laden with neurotoxin producing tissue. During a sting, as the spine enters the victim the skin covering is forced back, exposing the venom tissue lying along these grooves into the wound. There is generally very little trauma at the wound site and often it is even difficult to see the exact location of the sting. Symptoms of lionfish stings vary widely. Most victims will experience pain and swelling around the site of the sting. However, more severe symptoms can occur depending on the severity of the sting and the victim's reaction.

Photo courtesy of Ned DeLoach

In all cases, the immediate first aid treatment for stings is to soak the affected area in non-scalding hot water. Heat breaks down the venom and relieves the pain. For severe stings, medical attention is warranted. As of the printing of this book, no deaths have been attributed to lionfish stings. The final word on lionfish stings is prevention. Simple care and the use of proper equipment and procedures while catching and handling lionfish go a long way in preventing stings.

Collecting and Handling: Methods and Equipment

Lionfish are most often encountered while snorkeling or scuba diving. Their bold coloration and flowing fins are keys to proper identification. Collection of lionfish on a recreational basis is gaining favor with many recreational divers and spearfishers. However, proper techniques and equipment are essential for maximizing catch and minimizing stings during both the collecting and handling process.

Keep in mind that even though lionfish are non-native species and most countries are eager to encourage removals, existing rules, regulations, and gear restrictions must be followed. Be sure to check with local authorities or management agencies on allowable gear types and area restrictions before removing any lionfish.

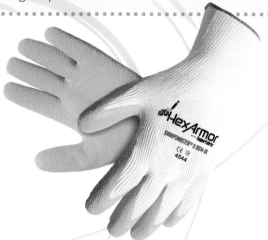

Gloves

An essential tool for handling and collecting lionfish are puncture resistant gloves. Though handling of lionfish should be minimal, the confidence and safety provided by these specialty gloves are worth the small initial investment. When shopping for gloves, be sure to look for puncture resistant gloves, not cut resistant. Kevlar gloves are great for warding off knife cuts, but don't do much for stopping sharply pointed objects like spines.

Photos courtesy of www.StuartCove.com

Spearing

Where allowed, spearing is often the most effective means of removing a large number of lionfish in a short amount of time. Lionfish that have not been subject to repeated capture attempts can usually be approached very closely and a well placed spear is more often than not quite effective. Standard or short length pole spears or Hawaiian slings are generally preferred and paralyzer-type tips can be most effective in disabling the fish until it can be bagged. Even though lionfish are typically quite bold and will allow a close approach, don't be fooled! They are ambush predators and can exhibit extremely rapid movement over short distances. Patience is the key. If you don't have a good shot, it is better to wait for the fish to move or wait for another day rather than missing the fish and helping it learn to avoid divers. Often a close look and then waiting a few minutes for the fish to reposition is all that is needed for a more successful capture.

Nets

 In areas that don't allow spearing, when time is not the important factor and for smaller fish, hand nets are certainly the most efficient lionfish collecting method. Typically, large, aluminum framed, clear vinyl nets used for collecting fish for aquariums are the most effective collection nets, however, mesh landing nets or lobster nets can also be used for larger fish. The key to using nets is to use them slowly. Rather than chasing lionfish around like butterflies, nets are used most effectively when lionfish are teased or coaxed into them. This requires patience and planning, but can also be great fun and very effective. When collecting with nets, use one net to strategically block off potential escape routes, then the second net to slowly herd and encourage the fish to swim into either open net on its own. Once inside a net, the two nets can be placed together, collectively closing off the openings. Fish can then be brought to the surface or transferred to a catch bag.

Catch bags

One of the most important goals in collecting lionfish is to avoid stings. This is best accomplished by knowing where the spines of the fish are at all times. For this reason, a clear dry bag makes a very effective catch bag. Even though spines are capable of protruding through the bag, they seldom do and even live lionfish are typically quite docile once inside the bag. Large bags can hold more than a dozen large lionfish. There are two main benefits for this type of collecting bag. First, the collector is aware of the location of lionfish in the bags at all times, which can be extremely useful when introducing newly captured individuals into a bag full of previously captured lionfish. A key step in the addition of new fish into the bag is to keep the bag on the bottom and move the previously captured fish toward the back of the bag before introducing newly captured fish. A second advantage of using dry bags is that they prevent the scent of freshly speared fish from attracting toothy critters.

Photo courtesy of www.StuartCove.com

Handling

We cannot stress enough that puncture resistant gloves are key for handling lionfish. Lionfish are members of the scorpionfish family and in addition to their venomous spines they also have very bony heads. Though not venomous, the bony protrusions on their heads and cheeks can rough up fingers and hands. The top and bottom of the fish, where the venomous spines are located, should be avoided. Wearing puncture proof gloves, a firm, one-handed grip across the front of the head, making sure you grasp both sides, is an effective way to hold lionfish while avoiding spines.

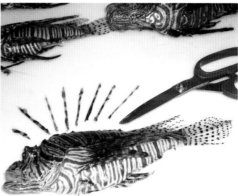

Scissors

An easy way to deal with lionfish spines is to simply cut them off. A good pair of kitchen shears or sea snips will make short work of the spines and once removed, there is little danger in getting stung. Even removing the sharp tips of the spines to render them dull can often suffice in preventing a poke. Once spines are removed, the fish can be handled easily.

Preparation

As you browse through the recipes in this book, you'll discover there are many ways to prepare lionfish. For an impressive presentation, the fish can be gutted, scaled and cooked whole. Lionfish can be butterflied and stuffed, filleted with skin on or skin off, or sectioned into bite-size pieces. There are certainly more methods and techniques for preparation than those presented in this book. Feel free to experiment and explore or find methods that work best for you.

Whole fish

When prepared whole, lionfish dishes can be quite dramatic. Flaring fins, prominent spines and bold coloration make for a striking presentation. For whole presentations you'll still need to remove the scales and gut the fish. To clean the fish, make an incision from the digestive tract opening on the bottom of the fish near the anal fin all the way forward to the bottom jaw. Reach into the gut cavity and remove the contents and cut free the gills from the head. Rinse the fish and gut cavity thoroughly. Scale your lionfish using a spoon or the dull side of a knife. Lionfish scales are quite small and easily removed, but they also end up every-where. Try scaling the fish under running water or in a bowl of water to reduce clean-up. Wash thoroughly after scaling.

Butterflying

For an alternative presentation style or for recipes that include stuffing, try butterflying your lionfish. As in preparing a whole fish, first gut and scale the lionfish. Next, using a very sharp knife, hold the fish on its back and make a cut on either side of the anal fin, angling in toward the backbone. Once these two cuts have been made, grasp the anal fin firmly and pull up and away from the fish to remove. The fish can then be sliced from the vent to the tail as needed to permit stuffing or to lay upright.

Filleting

There are many ways to fillet a fish. The method presented here may be a little more time consuming, but tends to yield the highest fillet weight. Most of the meat on a lionfish is located in what is referred to as the shoulder region of the fish. There is still substantial meat towards the tail, but like most fish, the fillet tends to get thinner near the tail. The stomach area of lionfish has less meat and more bone than the rest of the fish. For this reason, the fillet cut should take advantage of the meaty areas and avoid the bones.

To start the fillet process you'll need to make three cuts. First, with the fish laying flat on its side against the cutting board, lift the pectoral fin (not venomous). Starting at the top of the fish just in front of the first dorsal spine, cut at an angle down and behind the pectoral fin all the way to the stomach. Second, cut along the stomach from the end of the first cut to the tail.

Third, cut along the back just at the edge of the dorsal spines, from the beginning of your first cut to the top of the tail. Each cut should be just deep enough to cut through the lionfish's skin.

For skin-off lightly lift up the corner of skin near the head where the two cuts come together. Once you have a firm grip on the skin, simply pull down toward the tail. With fresh fish (colder is better) the skin should peel off easily leaving a nice view of the meat. For skin on fish, simply ignore this part. Turn the fish over and repeat the three cuts and skinning, if desired.

Next, starting at the front of the fish near the base of the spines, use repeated, short cuts parallel to the cutting board to slowly cut the fillet away from along the backbone. Move your cuts down toward the stomach and then toward the tail, freeing flesh from along the backbone. As you go, you can slowly lift the fillet up and by the time you reach the tail the fillet will be completely free from the backbone. Feel the stomach area of the fillet near the front of the fish and cut out any small bones remaining.

Repeat on the second side of the fish for two nice fillets. If the skin was left on, you'll want to scale the fillets before cooking.

Bites

For recipes requiring small pieces of fish, fillet your lionfish first, skin off, and cut the fillets into appropriately sized pieces.

Disposal

If the lionfish spines were not removed prior to cleaning, you will end up having leftover spines to deal with. One consideration when dealing with lionfish spines is that even though the venom is denatured by time and by cooking, the spines remain extremely sharp and require appropriate disposal. The last thing you'd want would be lionfish spines sticking out of a plastic trash bag and causing injury. A simple method of disposal is to place the spines inside a bottle or jar with a lid before placing in the trash. Grinding the spines up or returning them to deep water are also options or, for a unique presentation, place the individual spines on oven safe cookware and heat them in the oven at 350 degrees for 10-15 minutes. This will denature the venom and dry the colorful skin onto the spine making for extraordinary appetizer toothpicks and souvenirs!

RECIPES

The Caribbean's New Delicacy

Lionfish Carpaccio

4 fillets of lionfish

1/2 cup onions

1/2 cup olive oil

3 tablespoons capers

1/4 cup and 2 tablespoons lemon juice

1 tablespoon sugar

1/4 teaspoon pepper

1/4 teaspoon salt

1 baguette, thinly sliced

Thinly slice lionfish fillets so they are almost translucent. Thinly slice onion. Put the lionfish and the onion on a platter. Stir olive oil, lemon juice and sugar in a bowl together until combined. Add capers. Pour mixture on top of the lionfish and onion platter.

Serve with slices of baguette.

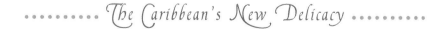

The Caribbean's New Delicacy

Lionfish Nachos

8 wonton wrappers*

½ cup oil

8 lionfish fillets

2 tablespoons sweet soy sauce*

2 tablespoons sweet Thai chili sauce*

1 tablespoon soy sauce

1 cup seaweed salad*

1/4 cup wasabi mayonnaise*

*Items can be found at oriental markets.

Place oil in a small frying pan and heat oil until hot. Place one wonton wrapper in at a time. Cook briefly until it starts to bubble. (Approximately 10 seconds.) Turn over and cook another 10 seconds. Remove and drain on kitchen towel.

Put wasabi mayonnaise into a squeeze bottle and set aside. Combine sweet soy sauce, sweet chili sauce and soy sauce together in a bowl and set aside. Spray skillet with non-stick cooking spray. Cook lionfish fillets in skillet over medium high heat for 2 to 3 minutes until flaky and tender. Cut or flake lionfish so it is in small pieces. Toss lionfish in soy sauce mixture.

Place lionfish on wonton wrappers, top with seaweed salad and drizzle with wasabi mayonnaise.

For a unique presentation, lionfish spines can be prepared and used for extraordinary appetizer toothpicks and souvenirs. Place the individual spines on oven safe cookware and heat them in the oven at 350 degrees for 10-15 minutes. This will denature the venom and dry the colorful skin onto the spine.

Spicy Lionfish Rosti

2 large potatoes
8 lionfish fillets
4 green onions diced
1 teaspoon fresh ginger grated
2 tablespoons fresh cilantro
2 teaspoons lemon juice
2 tablespoons vegetable oil
1 teaspoon salt
1/2 teaspoon cayenne pepper
Lemon
Cilantro for garnish

Peel and boil potatoes for 10 minutes. Set aside to cool. Chop lionfish into small pieces. Stir together diced onions, grated ginger, cilantro, lemon juice, salt and pepper in a bowl. Grate cooled potato into the fish mixture and stir together. Shape into 10 patties. Heat oil in skillet and cook patties for 3 minutes each side until brown and crisp. Remove and place on plate with paper towel. Transfer to serving dish squeeze with fresh lemon and garnish with cilantro.

...... *There is simply no "greener" fish to eat!* ......

Beer Battered Lionfish

with Dill Tartar Sauce

1 cup mayonnaise

1/4 cup dill pickle, minced

2 tablespoons lemon juice

1 tablespoon fresh dill

1 1/2 cups flour

1 cup beer

1 teaspoon garlic powder

1/2 teaspoon black pepper

8 fillets lionfish

Oil for frying

Combine first four ingredients in bowl and mix until blended. Combine flour, beer, garlic powder and pepper in a separate bowl. Cut lionfish fillets into strips. Heat oil in frying pan. When oil is hot, dredge fish through beer batter, covering the entire fish fillet. Put fish into hot oil and cook until golden brown. Turn fish with spatula until the other side is golden brown. Place a paper towel on a plate to absorb excess oil and transfer cooked fish to plate.

Serve with dill tartar sauce.

...... There is simply no "greener" fish to eat! ......

Bacon Wrapped Lionfish

1 lb lionfish fillets, cut into bite-size
  pieces
1 package sliced bacon

Preheat oven to 350 degrees. Cut bacon strips into 1/4 lengths. Wrap each lionfish piece in 1/4 strip of bacon and secure with a pick. Place bundles on a broiling tray or baking sheet. Bake at 350 degrees for 10-15 minutes or until desired bacon crispiness is achieved.

For a unique presentation, lionfish spines can be prepared and used for extraordinary appetizer toothpicks and souvenirs. Place the individual spines on oven safe cookware and heat them in the oven at 350 degrees for 10-15 minutes. This will denature the venom and dry the colorful skin onto the spine.

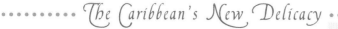
The Caribbean's New Delicacy

Thai Lionfish Cakes

1 lb lionfish
3 green onions
2 tablespoons cilantro
2 tablespoons red Thai curry paste
1 red chile
2 teaspoons lime zest
2 tablespoons vegetable oil
Sweet Thai chili sauce

Cut lionfish into chunks and pulse in food processor. Transfer to a bowl. Finely dice green onions and cilantro. Mince red chile. Combine green onions, cilantro, red Thai curry paste, red chile and fish. Stir together. Divide mixture into 12 portions and shape into balls, then flatten. Place the fish cakes on a plate with plastic wrap. If you need to put patties on top of each other place a layer of plastic wrap in between. Chill until firm between 1 – 2 hours. Heat oil in pan. Fry the fish cakes for 5-7 minutes until brown. Place on plate with paper towel to drain.

Serve with sweet Thai chile sauce.

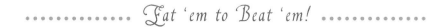
Eat 'em to Beat 'em!

Lionfish Fritters

1 cup lionfish
1 cup all purpose flour
1 teaspoon baking powder
1/4 cup onion diced
1/4 cup green pepper diced
1 teaspoon salt
1 teaspoon lime juice
1/2 teaspoon hot sauce
1 tablespoon thyme
1/2 cup water
Vegetable oil for frying

Sauce:
1/2 cup mayonnaise
1/2 cup ketchup
1 tablespoon Worcestershire sauce
1 teaspoon lime juice
1 teaspoon hot sauce

Spray pan with non-stick cooking spray. Heat pan and sauté fish for 2 minutes each side. Remove from pan, cool and flake fish in a bowl. Add the onion, green pepper, salt, limejuice, hot sauce and thyme. Sift together flour and baking powder. Add water to make batter. Stir together the fish mixture and batter.

Heat oil in deep skillet. Oil will be ready when a few drops of water sizzle in oil. Drop batter in hot oil by the teaspoonful. Cook until golden then turn. Cook until other side is golden; remove from pan onto paper towels. Serve with fritter sauce.

Lionfish Cakes

with Cilantro Lime Mayonnaise

1 1/2 cups fresh cilantro leaves (packed)

3 tablespoons fresh lime juice

1 teaspoon Dijon mustard

1/4 teaspoon hot pepper sauce

2 tablespoons sour cream

1 cup mayonnaise

1/2 teaspoon salt

2 large potatoes, peeled

1 lb lionfish fillets

1 small onion, peeled and grated

2 celery sticks, finely chopped

1 tablespoon parsley

1 tablespoon chives

1 tablespoon lemon juice

1 teaspoon salt

1/2 teaspoon hot sauce

2 eggs, lightly beaten

1/2 cup plain flour

2 cups fresh bread crumbs

Canola oil, to fry

Blend cilantro, limejuice, Dijon mustard and hot sauce in a food processor. Add sour cream and mayonnaise and process just to blend. Transfer to a squeeze bottle.

Cut the potatoes into rough chunks. Boil for 30 minutes, and then add the fish for another 10 minutes. Drain water, put mixture in bowl and mash together. Add chopped celery, grated onion, parsley, chives, lemon juice, salt and hot sauce. Mix together well. Use your hands to form into 8 fish cakes. Refrigerate for 30 minutes. Place flour in a bowl. Beat the eggs in a separate bowl. Place bread crumbs in separate bowl. Dip each patty in the flour, then in the egg mixture and lastly in the bread crumbs. Heat the oil in a heavy-based saucepan over medium-high heat. Add fish cakes and fry both sides until golden brown. Arrange 2 fish cakes on a plate, drizzle with cilantro lime mayonnaise.

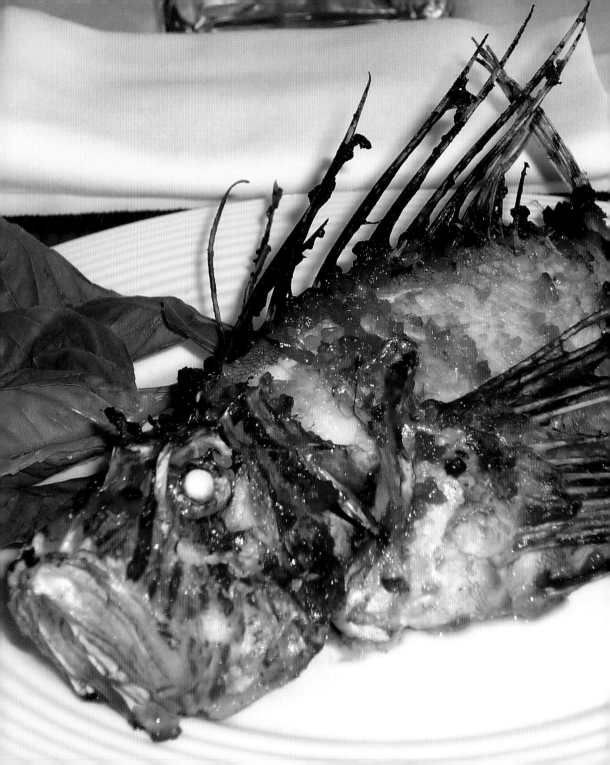

Baked Thai Lionfish

4 whole lionfish, cleaned and scaled*

1/2 cup fresh basil leaves

2 tablespoons peanut oil

2 tablespoons fish sauce*

2 cloves garlic, minced

1 teaspoon minced fresh ginger

2 red chile peppers, sliced diagonally

1 tablespoon brown sugar

1 tablespoon rice vinegar

2 tablespoons water

5 leaves basil

*Can be found at oriental markets.

Preheat oven to 375 degrees. Line a roasting pan with aluminum foil. Fill the cavity with basil leaves. Heat the peanut oil in a skillet. Place the lionfish in the skillet, and quickly brown on both sides, about 1 minute total. Place the fish into the roasting pan on its stomach so it is upright. In the skillet with the peanut oil, stir in the garlic, ginger, and chile peppers, sauté for 2 minutes. Stir in the sugar, rice vinegar, fish sauce and water. Bring to a simmer over medium-high heat until thickened to desired consistency. Pour the sauce over the lionfish. Bake in oven 20 minutes. Garnish with the remaining basil leaves to serve.

*Scale your lionfish using a spoon or the dull side of a knife. Lionfish scales are quite small and easily removed, but they also end up everywhere. Try scaling the fish under running water or in a bowl of water to reduce clean-up. Wash thoroughly after scaling.

Lionfish Tacos

8 Lionfish fillets
2 cups corn masa flour
1/2 teaspoon salt
1 1/8 cups water
1 1/2 cups flour
1 cup beer
1 teaspoon garlic powder
1/2 teaspoon pepper
1/2 cup mayonnaise
1/2 cup yogurt
1 clove garlic, peeled and minced

6 ripe tomatoes, peeled, seeded and diced
1/2 onion, minced
2 tablespoons cilantro leaves, chopped, stems removed
2 jalapeno peppers, seeded and chopped
1 1/2 teaspoons salt
Oil for deep-frying
1 head cabbage, green, shredded
1 lime, cut into wedges

Mix flour with favorite spices such as garlic powder, red or black ground pepper. Stir the flour mixture into the beer and mix until well blended. Wash fish by dipping in cold, lightly salted water or water with a little bit of lemon juice added. Be sure fish is completely dry before dipping into batter. Prepare salsa, mix garlic, tomatoes, onions, cilantro, jalapenos and salt. Reserve for later. Mix together corn masa, salt and water for 3 minutes until it becomes a dough ball. Separate the dough into 16 equally sized pieces. Form into flat balls. Place a floured (using corn masa) plastic bag down, put ball of dough on top, cover with another floured plastic bag, and roll the tortilla out. Slowly remove the top bag, flip it in your hand and remove the second plastic bag. Place the tortilla on a piece of wax paper. Continue with the next 15 tortillas. Put skillet on medium heat and place tortilla in pan. Once you begin to see bubbles appear take your spatula and flip it over and cook the other side.

Once the other side is a little brown remove it onto a plate or tortilla warmer. Put the vegetable oil into a deep skillet and bring to 375F. Place fish in a single layer--do not let pieces touch each other. Cook fish until batter is crispy and golden brown. To assemble on each tortilla layer the fish fillet, white sauce, salsa and cabbage. Top it off with a squeeze of lime. Fold tortilla over to serve.

Sweet Potato Encrusted Lionfish

1 sweet potato, grated
1 cup flour
1 teaspoon salt
1/2 teaspoon black pepper
8 lionfish fillets
3 egg whites
3 tablespoons coconut oil

Peel and grate the sweet potato, place in a shallow bowl, and set aside. Place the flour, salt and pepper in a separate bowl. In another separate bowl, beat the egg whites and set aside. Heat your sauté pan and add the oil. Dip the fish into the flour, then in the egg, and last into the grated sweet potato. Place in a heated pan and sauté for 2 minutes on each side until crispy and brown.

Eat 'em to Beat 'em!

Coconut Panko Lionfish
with Mango Curry Sauce

Mango Curry Sauce:

2 mangos
1 small onion, diced
1 tablespoon curry powder
1 tablespoon turmeric
1 teaspoon cumin
1 teaspoon coriander
1/4 teaspoon salt
1/2 teaspoon hot sauce

Combine all ingredients for the mango curry in a saucepan. Cook until mango and onions are tender and soft, about 10 minutes. Blend in a food processor until smooth. Set aside.

3 tablespoons all purpose flour
1 teaspoon salt
1/2 teaspoon ground ginger
1 egg
2 tablespoons liquid honey
1/2 cup grated coconut
1/2 cup panko bread crumbs
8 lionfish fillets
4 cups vegetable oil for frying
1 lime, cut into wedges

Stir flour with salt and ginger in a wide shallow bowl. Whisk egg with honey in a separate bowl. In another bowl stir coconut and panko. Coat lionfish in flour, shaking off excess. Dip in egg mixture then dredge through coconut mixture. Set aside on wax paper lined bake sheet until all lionfish are coated. Heat oil in a frying pan. Place fillets in oil for 2 minutes per side, until they are golden. Remove from oil, place on paper towel lined plate. Serve with mango curry sauce and lime wedge.

Blackened Lionfish

8 lionfish fillets

1 tablespoon paprika

1 tablespoon salt

1 1/2 tablespoons black pepper

1 teaspoon cayenne

1 1/2 teaspoons oregano

1 1/2 teaspoons onion powder

1 1/2 teaspoons garlic powder

1/4 cup butter

Mix together all dry ingredients.

Pat onto fillets.

Melt butter in a frying pan.

Cook fish 2 minutes per side.

The Caribbean's New Delicacy

Baked Lionfish

with Olives, Tomatoes and Capers

8 lionfish fillets

8 cherry tomatoes, cut in half

16 black olives, halved

2 tablespoons capers

4 thyme sprigs

4 tablespoons olive oil

2 tablespoons balsamic vinegar

Preheat oven to 400 degrees. Grease roasting pan with 2 tablespoons olive oil. Reserve remainder of olive oil. Place fish in roasting pan with tomatoes, olives, capers and thyme. Drizzle with remaining olive oil. Bake in oven 15 minutes.

Remove from oven and drizzle with balsamic vinegar.

...... *There is simply no "greener" fish to eat!* ......

Spicy Lionfish
with Dill Sauce

2 teaspoons lemon juice

1/4 cup sour cream

2 tablespoons mayonnaise

1 tablespoon fresh dill

1 tablespoon fresh chives

1 tablespoon capers

1/4 teaspoon salt

8 lionfish fillets

1 tablespoon Creole seasoning

2 tablespoons butter

In a small bowl, squeeze juice from 1 lemon. In a medium bowl, combine 2 teaspoons of the lemon juice, the sour cream, mayonnaise, fresh dill, fresh chives and capers. Blend until well combined.

Sprinkle Creole seasoning on fillets. Heat butter in skillet. Pan fry fillets 2 minutes each side until browned.

Place cooked fillets on a plate and serve with dill sauce.

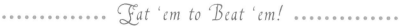

Eat 'em to Beat 'em!

Asian Lionfish

1 teaspoon orange zest
Juice from 1 orange
1 tablespoon grated fresh ginger
1 teaspoon minced garlic
3 tablespoons rice wine vinegar
3 tablespoons soy sauce
1 teaspoon red chile pepper
2 tablespoons sesame oil
2 tablespoons fresh cilantro
1 tablespoon sesame seeds
8 lionfish fillets

Take orange and zest the rind. Use the same orange and squeeze for fresh juice. Grate ginger, and mince garlic. In a plastic bag combine zest, orange juice, ginger, garlic, chile pepper, vinegar and soy sauce. Add lionfish, close Ziploc bag and refrigerate. Marinate for 30 minutes, turning once.

Remove lionfish from marinade, and reserve marinade. Heat oil in a large skillet over medium high heat. Add lionfish and cook 2 minutes. Turn lionfish and cook another 2 minutes. Transfer lionfish to plate. In pan, add marinade and cook over medium heat. Reduce by half. Drizzle over lionfish, garnish with cilantro and sesame seeds.

Can be served on a bed of steamed spinach with jasmine rice.

Lionfish Veracruz

1/4 cup olive oil
1/2 cup diced onions
2 garlic cloves
1 can diced tomatoes
1/4 cup green olives, halved
2 tablespoons capers
1/4 teaspoon dried oregano
1/4 teaspoon pepper
1 teaspoon salt
1/2 teaspoon garlic powder
8 lionfish fillets
2 teaspoons butter

Heat 2 tablespoons oil in a skillet over medium high heat. Sauté onions until tender – about 3 minutes. Add garlic and sauté 15 seconds. Add tomatoes, olives, and capers. Bring to a boil and reduce heat. Add oregano and simmer 5 minutes.

Sprinkle lionfish with salt, pepper and garlic powder. Melt butter with 2 tablespoons olive oil in a separate pan over medium high heat. Add lionfish and cook 2 minutes on each side. Transfer lionfish to plates.

Serve sauce on top of fish.

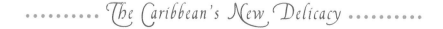

The Caribbean's New Delicacy

Lionfish

with Sweet Thai Chili Sauce

2 eggs
1 cup flour
1 cup panko bread crumbs
8 lionfish fillets
Canola oil for frying
Sweet Thai chili sauce
Lime, cut into wedges

Beat eggs in bowl. Add flour and panko bread crumbs to two separate bowls. Dredge lionfish through flour, then eggs then panko. Transfer to a plate and refrigerate while oil is heating.

Heat oil in a skillet. Oil is hot enough when a drop of water sizzles when put in the oil. Put fish in pan and cook 2 minutes per side, until golden brown. Transfer to a plate lined with paper towel to soak up oil. Transfer to serving plate and serve with sweet Thai chili sauce and wedge of lime.

...... There is simply no "greener" fish to eat! ......

Mango Salsa Lionfish

8 lionfish fillets
2 teaspoons garlic powder
1 1/2 teaspoons salt
1/2 teaspoon pepper
2 limes
1/4 cup fresh cilantro
1 cup mango diced
1/4 cup onion
Hot sauce to taste

Squeeze juice from 1 lime on fillets. Season with 1 teaspoon salt, pepper and garlic powder. Refrigerate for 30 minutes.

Combine mango, onion, cilantro, juice from 1 lime, 1/2 teaspoon salt and hot sauce. Set aside. Heat 1 tablespoon of olive oil in skillet on medium high heat. Remove fish from refrigerator, place in skillet. Cook 2 minutes per side, until flaky.

Place fish on plate, spoon mango salsa over fish.

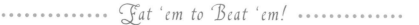

Eat 'em to Beat 'em!

Pan Seared Lionfish
with Red Thai Curry Sauce

4 tablespoons peanut oil

1/2 medium onion diced

1 clove garlic, peeled and diced

1 teaspoon Thai red curry paste

1/2 cup coconut milk

1/2 cup chicken stock

1 tablespoon fish sauce

1 teaspoon sugar

1/2 teaspoon salt

1 tablespoon cornstarch

1 tablespoon water

1 tablespoon lemon juice

4 basil leaves

1/2 teaspoon pepper

8 lionfish fillets

Heat 2 tablespoons of oil in saucepan on medium high heat. Add onions and sauté 5 minutes. Add the Thai red curry paste and garlic and cook for one minute stirring. Add the coconut milk, chicken stock, fish sauce, sugar and ¼ teaspoon of salt. Bring to a boil. Cover with lid, reduce heat and simmer for 15 minutes.

Combine the cornstarch and water in a bowl. Add the cornstarch mixture to the saucepan and stir continuously until the curry thickens, then stir in the lemon juice and basil. Leave on low heat while cooking fish.

Heat remaining 2 tablespoons of oil in skillet. Season fish with remaining salt and pepper. Sauté fish in skillet for 2 minutes per side. Transfer to plate and spoon Thai red curry sauce on top of fish.

Orange Ginger Lionfish

8 lionfish fillets

2 oranges, juiced

2 tablespoons fresh lime juice

1 tablespoon brown sugar

2 tablespoons soy sauce

1 teaspoon sesame oil

1 pinch red pepper flakes

2 teaspoons finely chopped fresh ginger

2 oranges - peeled and chopped

2 tablespoons cilantro

2 green onions, finely chopped

Preheat the oven to 375 degrees. Arrange the lionfish fillet in a single layer in the bottom of a lightly greased and shallow baking dish. In a medium bowl, stir together the orange juice, lime juice, brown sugar, soy sauce and sesame oil. Mix in the red pepper flakes, ginger and chopped oranges. Pour over the lionfish in the dish.

Bake uncovered for about 15 minutes in the preheated oven, or until fish is opaque. Transfer fillets to serving plates and spoon the sauce over them.

Garnish with cilantro and onions.

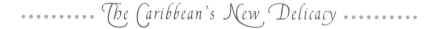

The Caribbean's New Delicacy

Pesto Lionfish

8 lionfish fillets

Non-stick cooking spray or
   olive oil

Pesto (can use store bought, but
recipe is included)

2 cups fresh basil, packed

1/2 cup grated Parmesan cheese

1/2 cup extra virgin olive oil

1/3 cup pine nuts

3 garlic cloves

1 teaspoon salt

1/2 teaspoon pepper

Preheat oven to 375 degrees. To make the pesto, combine basil and pine nuts in a food processor and pulse a few times. Add garlic and pulse a few more times. Add the olive oil in a steady stream while the processor is on. You may have to stop a couple times to scrape the sides and make sure the ingredients are combined. Add the grated Parmesan, salt and pepper. Pulse until blended.

Spray or oil baking pan. Put lionfish fillets in pan, spoon 2 tablespoons of pesto on each fillet. Bake for 15 minutes.

...... *There is simply no "greener" fish to eat!* ......

Grilled Lionfish Packets

Non-stick cooking spray

2 carrots

2 stalks celery

2 plantains

1 medium onion

1 tomato

4 lionfish fillets

8 tablespoons butter

8 tablespoons lemon juice

4 teaspoons garlic powder

1/2 teaspoon salt

Hot sauce to taste

Aluminum foil

Lay two pieces of foil on the counter overlapping in the middle. Make four of these, so you will need eight pieces of foil. Spray foil on ingredient side with non-stick cooking spray. Peel carrots and cut in half, then in half again. Slice carrots so you have half moon slices. Divide between the four foil packets. Cut celery in slices. Divide between the packets. Cut plantain in half, then in half lengthwise. Make half moon slices and divide between the packets. Dice onion and tomato and divide between the packets. Lay whole fillet on top of vegetables, one per packet. Put 2 tablespoons of butter in each packet. Pour over ingredients 2 tablespoons of lemon juice per packet. Sprinkle each packet with 1 teaspoon garlic powder, 1/8 teaspoon salt and hot sauce. Fold foil lengthwise towards the center. Fold over twice closing the center, being careful lemon juice doesn't run out the sides. Fold each end towards the center. Your packet should look like a canoe.

Put on the barbeque grill on medium high for 15 – 20 minutes until vegetables are cooked.

Lionfish Curry

3 tablespoons oil

4 cloves garlic minced

3 medium onions

1 tablespoon turmeric

1 teaspoon cumin

1 teaspoon coriander

2 tablespoons hot madras curry powder

1 tablespoon mild madras curry powder

1 inch fresh ginger root, finely grated

1 tomato finely diced

2 tablespoons fresh lime juice

1/2 to 1 cup fresh cilantro

2 cans coconut milk

8 fillets lionfish

1 bag frozen peas

Chop onions and put in food processor. Pulse until finely diced. Heat oil in pot on high heat until hot. Add garlic to oil, and reduce heat to medium. Sauté for 1 minute. Stir onions into garlic and oil until coated. Cover and simmer for 15 minutes until onions are opaque. Add turmeric, and sauté for 30 seconds. Add cumin, coriander and curry powder. Simmer for 10 minutes. Add fresh ginger, 1 cup of coconut milk and cilantro. Simmer on low for 1 hour. Add lime juice and tomatoes, and continue to simmer for 10 minutes. Add the rest of coconut milk and simmer for 1 hour on low. Add the peas and cook for 5 minutes. Cut the lionfish into 2 inch x 2 inch pieces. Place the lionfish into the liquid and cook on low, and then simmer until opaque and flaky. Try to avoid stirring so as not to break up the fish fillets. Serve over rice or with chapatti.

This can also served with Indian Chapatti Bread. For recipe, see page 121.

Crab Stuffed Lionfish

Stuffing:

8 ounces crabmeat

1 egg beaten

1/2 cup plain bread crumbs

2 tablespoons chopped celery

2 tablespoons diced onion

1/2 cup fresh parsley

2 tablespoons mayonnaise

1/2 teaspoon Old Bay seasoning

1/2 teaspoon hot sauce

8 lionfish fillets

Non-stick cooking spray

Sauce:

2 tablespoons butter

2 tablespoons flour

1 teaspoon dry mustard powder

1 cup milk

1/2 teaspoon salt

1/4 teaspoon white pepper

1/2 cup grated Swiss cheese

Preheat oven to 400 degrees. Spray casserole dish with non-stick cooking spray. In a bowl mix together all ingredients for the stuffing. Place 1/8 of the mixture in the center of each fillet. Roll fillet and place seam side down in casserole dish. Bake for 20 minutes.

While fish is baking, heat butter in saucepan. Add flour and dry mustard, salt and pepper. Cook over low heat until bubbly, 1 - 2 minutes. Slowly whisk in milk. Add grated cheese and cook until cheese is melted and sauce is thickened. When fish is done, place on serving plate and spoon sauce on top. Garnish with parsley.

Lionfish Seafood Crepes

Crepes: (Makes 10 crepes)
1 1/2 cups flour
1/2 teaspoon baking powder
1/2 teaspoon salt
Non-stick cooking spray
2 cups milk
2 tablespoons butter, melted
2 eggs

Spray small skillet with cooking spray. Heat skillet. Pour ¼ cup of batter in hot pan. Rotate pan so the entire surface is covered with batter in a thin coat. Cook until golden. Run spatula around outer edge of crepe. Turn over and cook other side until golden. Place crepe on a plate with wax paper. Layer crepes between wax paper.

Filling:

4 lionfish fillets, cut into pieces
1 lobster tail, shelled cut into chunks
8 large shrimp, peeled and deveined
2 cups sliced mushrooms
4 green onions
1 tablespoon parsley
1 tablespoon minced garlic

4 tablespoons butter
2 tablespoons flour
1/4 teaspoon salt
1/4 teaspoon white pepper
1 cup milk
1/2 cup Swiss cheese
Fresh parsley

Melt 2 tablespoons butter in sauté pan. Sauté mushrooms for 2 minutes. Add parsley and garlic and green onions, cook for 1 minute. Add lobster chunks, shrimp and lionfish. Set aside. Combine flour, salt and pepper. Melt remaining 2 tablespoons butter in a second pan. Add flour and spices to butter. Stir and cook until bubbly. Slowly add milk and whisk until smooth. Add Swiss cheese. Stir until melted. Combine the fish mixture with the sauce. Place crepes on a plate and ladle filling down the center of the crepe. Roll crepe and place seam side down on the plate. Continue rolling the rest of the crepes. Garnish with fresh parsley. Serve two per plate for main course or one for appetizer.

Lionfish Pie

4 tablespoons butter

1 cup mushrooms

2 green onions diced

1 can cream of mushroom soup
with ½ can milk

1 teaspoon garlic powder

1 teaspoon thyme

1/2 teaspoon salt

1/4 teaspoon pepper

1 lb lionfish

4 large potatoes

2/3-cup milk

Preheat oven to 350 degrees. Peel and cut potatoes. Put in a pot with water covering potatoes. Boil potatoes 30 – 45 minutes. Drain water and combine potatoes with 2 tablespoons butter and milk. Mash together and set aside.

Heat 2 tablespoons butter in frying pan. Add mushrooms and onions. Sauté 3 minutes. Add garlic powder, thyme, salt and pepper. Cook 1 minute. Add fish and cook until fish is opaque and flaky. Add cream of mushroom soup and half can of milk. Transfer to casserole dish. Top with mashed potatoes. Bake in oven for 30 minutes until top is golden brown.

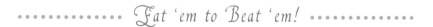

· · · · · · · · · · · · · *Eat 'em to Beat 'em!* · · · · · · · · · · · · ·

Baked Lionfish

8 lionfish fillets

2 cups spinach

1 cup bread crumbs

2 tablespoons chopped parsley

1 teaspoon lemon zest

Lemon juice from ½ lemon

1/4 cup Parmesan cheese grated

1 teaspoon vegetable oil

1/2 teaspoon salt

1/4 teaspoon pepper

Preheat oven to 400 degrees. Place lionfish in oven safe dish. Chop spinach leaves and arrange on top of fish. Combine bread crumbs, parsley, lemon zest, lemon juice, Parmesan cheese, oil and salt and pepper in bowl. Spoon bread crumb mixture over fish.

Bake for 15 minutes.

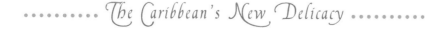

The Caribbean's New Delicacy

Coconut Baked Lionfish

2 teaspoons grated ginger

4 red chilies

8 lionfish fillets

2 cups coconut milk

Limejuice from 3 limes

4 tablespoons fish sauce

2 tablespoons sesame oil

3 tablespoons fresh cilantro

Preheat oven to 375 degrees. Place lionfish in an ovenproof dish. Combine coconut milk, lime juice, fish sauce, sesame oil, grated ginger and diced chilies and cilantro. Pour over lionfish.

Bake in oven for 15 minutes. Garnish with fresh cilantro.

...... *There is simply no "greener" fish to eat!* ......

Lionfish Chowder

2 tablespoons butter

2 cups chopped onion

1 stalk celery, chopped

1/8 teaspoon Old Bay Seasoning

Salt to taste

Ground black pepper to taste

4 cups chicken stock

4 cups diced potatoes

1 pounds lionfish, cut into pieces

1 pound bay scallops

1 can corn

1 cup clam juice

1/2 cup all-purpose flour

2 cans evaporated milk

Melt butter in large pot. Add onions, celery, Old Bay Seasoning, salt and pepper, and cook for 5 minutes. Add chicken stock and potatoes. Cook for 10 minutes. Add fish and bay scallops. Cook for an additional 10 minutes. Add corn. Combine clam juice and flour, and add to pot. Remove from heat and add evaporated milk.

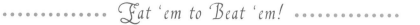

Eat 'em to Beat 'em!

Baked Lionfish

with Garlic Mayonnaise

1 cup mayonnaise

3 cloves garlic minced

2 chopped green onions

2 tablespoons fresh parsley

1 tablespoon lemon juice

Preheat oven to 375 degrees. Mix together mayonnaise, garlic, green onions, parsley, and lemon juice. Grease baking dish. Lay lionfish in baking dish. Spread garlic mayonnaise over fish and bake for 15 minutes.

The Caribbean's New Delicacy

Lionfish Seafood Lasagna

No-cook lasagna noodles

3/4 cup butter

2 cloves garlic minced

1 tablespoon dry parsley

1 teaspoon salt

1/2 teaspoon white pepper

3/4 cup flour

2 cups milk

2 cups cream

2 cups Parmesan cheese grated

2 tablespoons vegetable oil

1/2 lb shrimp

1 6-ounce can of crab

4 lionfish fillets

1/2 lb lobster

1 box frozen spinach, thawed and squeezed dry

16 oz mozzarella cheese grated

2 tablespoons fresh parsley

Preheat oven 375 degrees. Combine garlic, parsley, salt, pepper and flour in bowl. Add butter to sauce pan. Melt until bubbly. Whisk flour mixture in saucepan, cook until bubbly. Slowly whisk in milk and cream. Add Parmesan cheese and cook until thickened. Chop seafood into pieces. Heat 2 tablespoons oil in a separate pan. Sauté lobster and shrimp for 1 minute. Add fish, sauté for 1 minute, and add crab. Combine sauce and seafood. Ladle enough sauce to cover bottom of lasagna pan. Layer with noodles. Layer sauce, noodles, spinach and mozzarella cheese. Continue layering until done. Cover with aluminum foil bake for 30 minutes. Remove foil and bake an additional 10 minutes. Remove from oven, cover with foil and let rest 10 minutes. Garnish with fresh parsley.

Thai Lionfish

1 tablespoon peanut oil

3 teaspoons sesame oil

1 teaspoon ginger peeled and grated

3 garlic cloves, minced

1 tablespoon fish sauce

1 tablespoon soy sauce

Juice of 1 lemon

2 green onions

8 lionfish fillets

Sesame seeds

Put peanut oil and 1 teaspoon sesame oil in pan. Sauté ginger and garlic for 1 minute. Add fish sauce, soy sauce, lemon juice and green onions. Simmer for 5 minutes. In a separate pan, heat remaining sesame oil to hot. Sear lionfish in pan 2 minutes per side. Transfer to a serving dish and pour sauce over fish. Garnish with sesame seeds.

······ There is simply no "greener" fish to eat! ······

Avocado Salsa Lionfish

1 medium tomato, diced

1 avocado, cubed

1 small onion, diced

4 limes, juiced

1/2 cup cilantro

1 jalapeno pepper, seeded and
   diced

1 teaspoon salt

8 lionfish fillets

Juice from 2 limes

1/2 teaspoon pepper

2 teaspoons garlic powder

2 tablespoons olive oil

Combine tomato, avocado, onion, lime juice, cilantro jalapeno pepper and 1/2 teaspoon salt in a bowl. Set aside. Squeeze the juice of two limes over the lionfish. Season lionfish with 1/2 teaspoon salt, pepper and garlic powder. Heat oil in pan. Cook fish for 2 minutes per side until golden. Transfer to serving dish and spoon avocado salsa over fish.

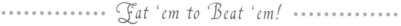

Eat 'em to Beat 'em!

Sweet and Spicy Lionfish

4 whole lionfish

1/2 cup fresh basil

4 limes

4 tablespoons oyster sauce

4 tablespoons soy sauce

8-10 cloves garlic, minced or
   pressed

1 tablespoon fish sauce

3 tablespoons brown sugar,

1 tablespoon lime juice

4 red chilies, seeded and sliced
   into thin slices

Preheat oven to 375 degrees. Put two slices of lime and two basil leaves in the cavity of the fish. Combine oyster sauce, soy sauce, garlic, fish sauce, brown sugar, lime juice and red chilies in a saucepan. Cook on medium low for 5 minutes. Divide sauce between four fish, taking care to put some sauce in each cavity.

Place in an ovenproof dish and bake for 20 – 25 minutes.

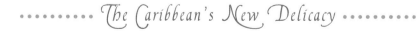

The Caribbean's New Delicacy

Lionfish Seafood in a Puff Pastry

6 puff pastry shells

1 cup shrimp

1 cup lobster

1 cup bay scallops

4 lionfish fillets

4 tablespoons butter

3 tablespoons garlic, minced

1/2 teaspoon salt

1 teaspoon dried parsley

2 tablespoons flour

1 cup milk

6 fresh parsley sprigs

Prepare puff pastry shells per instruction on back of box. Set aside. In a saucepan, melt 2 tablespoons butter over medium heat. Add 2 tablespoons garlic, salt and parsley. Cook for 1 minute. Add flour and cook until bubbly. Whisk milk into mixture. Cook until slightly thickened, and set aside. Chop shrimp, lobster and lionfish into 1-inch pieces. In a frying pan, melt 2 tablespoons butter. Add 1 tablespoon garlic and cook for 2 minutes on medium heat. Add shrimp, lobster, lionfish and scallops. Cook for 4-5 minutes, until seafood is opaque and fish is flaky. Add sauce to pan, and cook for 2 minutes. Set puff pastry shells on individual plates. Divide mixture between the six puff pastry shells, garnish with fresh parsley sprigs.

Lionfish Amandine

8 fillets lionfish

1/2 cup coarsely ground almonds

1/4 cup butter, softened

1/2 teaspoon salt

1/2 teaspoon paprika

2 tablespoon lemon juice

1 lemon

Fresh parsley for garnish

Heat oven to 350. Grease baking dish. Place lionfish in baking dish. Pour lemon juice over fish. Place almonds in a food processor and process until coarsely ground. Combine almonds, butter, salt and paprika, and spoon over fish. Bake uncovered for 20 minutes.

Cut lemon into wedges, chop parsley. Transfer fish to plate and garnish with lemon wedge and parsley.

•••••• There is simply no "greener" fish to eat! ••••••

Spicy Cornmeal Lionfish

8 fillets lionfish

3/4 cups fine yellow cornmeal

1/4 cup flour

1/2 teaspoon salt

1/2 teaspoon garlic powder

1/2 teaspoon dried parsley

1/2 teaspoon cayenne

1/2 teaspoon pepper

3 drops hot sauce

2 eggs

3 tablespoons butter, melted

Preheat oven to 375 degrees. Combine cornmeal, flour, salt, garlic powder, parsley, cayenne and pepper in a shallow bowl. Combine eggs and hot sauce. Dip fish in egg, then in cornmeal mixture. Place on un-greased baking sheet and drizzle with butter.

Cook for 10 – 12 minutes.

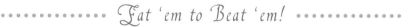

Eat 'em to Beat 'em!

Lionfish Ceviche

8 lionfish fillets

1 tomato

2 scotch bonnet peppers

1/2 onion

8 limes

1/4 teaspoon salt

2 tablespoons finely chopped
   cilantro

Dice fish into 1-inch pieces and place in a shallow dish.

In a small bowl, juice the 8 limes. Add the lime juice to fish and marinate 1 1/2 hours.

Dice the onions, tomatoes and scotch bonnet peppers, and add to fish mixture. Stir in salt and cilantro. Cover and place back in refrigerator for 30 minutes.

Remove from refrigerator and serve.

The Caribbean's New Delicacy

Hawaiian Lionfish

8 lionfish fillets

3 eggs, beaten

1 cup chopped toasted almonds

1 cup flaked coconut

1 tablespoon sesame seeds

1 tablespoon brown sugar

1 (15 ounce) can crushed
pineapple, drained

1/2 cup chopped onion

Preheat oven to 350 degrees. Grease a large baking dish. Place almonds in a food processor and process until coarse. Place the beaten eggs in a shallow dish. Mix the almonds, coconut, sesame seeds and brown sugar together in a mixing bowl. Stir the pineapple and onion together in a separate bowl. Dip each lionfish fillet into the beaten egg and then press into the almond mixture. Place the coated lionfish into the prepared dish. Spread the pineapple mixture over the coated fillets. Sprinkle some almond mixture over pineapple mixture.

Bake in the preheated oven until the fish flakes easily with a fork, about 20 – 30 minutes.

Almond Crusted Lionfish

8 lionfish fillets

2 eggs

1 teaspoon pepper

1 teaspoon garlic powder

1 cup ground almonds

1 cup freshly grated Parmesan cheese

1/4 cup all-purpose flour

6 tablespoons butter

1 teaspoon salt

Parsley for garnish

8 lemon wedges

Preheat oven to 375 degrees. In a small bowl, beat eggs. Combine pepper, garlic powder, almonds and Parmesan cheese in a separate bowl. Place flour in third bowl. Dredge fish through flour and shake off excess. Dip in the eggs then coat in almond mixture. Heat butter in large skillet on medium high heat. Cook lionfish 2 minutes per side until golden brown.

Place fish on a plate and squeeze lemon over fish. Sprinkle with parsley.

...... There is simply no "greener" fish to eat! ......

Steamed Lionfish

8 lionfish fillets

2 limes

1 teaspoon garlic powder

1/2 teaspoon dried thyme

1/4 teaspoon salt

1/8 teaspoon ground black pepper

1 large onion, sliced

1 green bell pepper, thinly sliced

1 can diced tomatoes

Preheat oven to 375 degrees. Squeeze lime juice over fillets. Season fillets with garlic powder, thyme, salt and pepper, and refrigerate lionfish for 1 hour. Remove from refrigerator and place fish in a baking dish.

Top with onion, green pepper and tomatoes, and bake for 20 minutes.

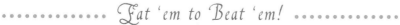

Eat 'em to Beat 'em!

Garlic Lemon Lionfish

8 lionfish fillets
3 tablespoon fresh lemon juice
1 tablespoon butter, melted
1 teaspoon garlic powder
1 tablespoon fresh parsley
1/4 teaspoon pepper
1/4 teaspoon salt

Preheat oven to 350 degrees. Place fish in a greased oven proof dish. Cover with lemon juice, melted butter garlic, parsley, salt, and pepper.

Bake for 20 minutes until opaque and flaky.

The Caribbean's New Delicacy

Macadamia Nut Lionfish
with Roasted Red Pepper Sauce

1 20 oz jar of roasted red peppers
1 teaspoon garlic minced
1 tablespoon balsamic vinegar
1 teaspoon salt
1/4 teaspoon cayenne
3 tablespoons tomato sauce
1/4 teaspoon black pepper
3 tablespoons olive oil
8 lionfish fillets
1 1/4 cups coarsely ground
   roasted macadamia nuts
1/2 cup panko breadcrumbs
1/2 cup flour
2 eggs
Vegetable oil for frying

Combine the first 8 ingredients in a food processor and blend together. Put mixture in a saucepan over medium heat, and heat thoroughly. Grind roasted macadamia nuts in a food processor. Place ground nuts in a bowl and add panko. Mix together. Put flour and eggs in two separate bowls. Dip fish into flour and shake off excess. Dip into egg and then into macadamia nut mixture. Set on an empty plate, and continue with the remainder of fish.

Heat oil in skillet. Cook fish 2 minutes per side until golden brown. Put on serving plate and spoon red pepper sauce on top of fillet.

...... There is simply no "greener" fish to eat! ......

Macadamia Coconut Lionfish
with Pineapple Salsa

1 1/2 cups chopped pineapple
1 small onion diced
1 1/2 tablespoons lime juice
1 teaspoon minced jalapeno
1 teaspoon fresh grated ginger
2 tablespoon fresh cilantro
1/4 teaspoon salt
1/4 cup coconut
1/4 cup ground roasted
   macadamia nuts
1/4 cup panko breadcrumbs
4 tablespoon flour
2 eggs
8 lionfish fillets
Vegetable oil for frying
Cilantro for garnish

Combine first seven ingredients. Mix together and set aside. Combine coconut, nuts and panko in one bowl. Put flour and eggs in two other separate bowls. Dredge fish in flour and shake off excess. Dip in egg mixture and coat in nut mixture. Continue with all fillets. Heat oil in pan. Oil will be ready when a few drops of water sizzle in pan. Cook fish in pan 2 minutes each side until golden brown. Remove onto plate and spoon pineapple salsa over fish. Garnish with fresh cilantro.

Eat 'em to Beat 'em!

Indian Chapatti Bread

1 1/4 cup whole-wheat flour, preferably Indian

1/4 teaspoon salt

1/2 cup lukewarm water, use more when needed

1 tablespoon olive oil

2 teaspoons butter

Mix flour, salt and water together to make soft dough. Add more water if dough is too dry. Use olive oil to grease surface. Knead dough on greased surface until smooth. Set dough aside and cover with a damp cloth for 30 minutes.

Divide dough into 8 equal portions. Make a ball and press flat. Dip ball into dry whole wheat flour on both sides. Roll into a 6 inch circle. Heat skillet on medium high. Ideally a cast iron skillet is the best. Skillet is hot enough when a few drops of water sizzles in the pan. Place chapatti in skillet. Once the chapatti starts to bubble turn over. Turn again after a few seconds. Take a flat spatula and press lightly on the puffed parts. Turn over again. There should be light brown spots on both sides. Butter the chapatti. Put paper towel in bottom of container, put chapatti in container, and cover while continuing to make the rest of the chapatti.

NUTRITIONAL VALUE

Lionfish are not only a delicious and environmentally-friendly food choice, they're also nutritious. The health benefits of consuming sea food, and particularly fish, for promoting healthy hearts and circulatory systems, have been widely publicized in recent years. Consuming foods high in Omega 3 fats and low in Omega 6 fats can lower bad cholesterol (LDL) while raising good cholesterol (HDL). A recent nutritional study found lionfish to be high in lean protein and an excellent source of important Omega 3 fats. The information presented below comes from an independent analysis conducted by the Microbac Laboratories, Inc testing and research facility in Wilson, North Carolina.

*% Daily Value (DV) based on a 2,000 calorie diet

Nutrition Facts (Lionfish)

Serving Size	100 grams	
Amount Per Serving		
Calories 80		Cal from Fat 0
		% Daily Value*
Total Fat 0g	2%	
Saturated Fat 0g	0%	
Trans Fat 0g		
Cholesterol 50mg	17%	
Sodium 60mg	3%	
Total Carbohydrate 0g	0%	
Dietary Fiber 2g	8%	
Sugars 1g		
Protein 18g		
Vitamin A 0%	Vitamin C 0%	
Calcium 25%	Iron 0%	

*Percent Daily values are based on a 2,000 Calorie diet. Your daily values may be higher or lower depending on your calorie needs.

About the Authors

Photo by Laura Garcia Bartenfelder

Tricia Ferguson

This book would not be possible without the generous contribution and unique culinary expertise of Tricia Ferguson. Born in Canada and now residing in Eleuthera, Bahamas, Tricia and her husband David are avid snorkelers, divers and marine life enthusiasts. As a personal "chef to the stars" on Bahamas' Harbour Island, Tricia used her expertise with seafood to adapt, modify and develop compatible gourmet tastes and novel combinations for the 45 recipes in this volume. Her respect for the marine environment motivates her to devote countless hours refining her dishes to promote lionfish as the new Caribbean delicacy.

Lad Akins

Lad Akins is the Founding Executive Director of REEF and led the organization in that capacity for 16 years, helping to design and develop the organization's widely recognized marine conservation programs. In 2005, he stepped down to focus his efforts solely on the lionfish invasion. A professional diver and Coast Guard Captain, Lad has successfully bridged the gap between science, academia, management, commercial interests and the public. His broad perspective includes serving on numerous state, federal and international boards, panels and working groups, discovering and describing new species of fish, conducting research as an aquanaut in the Aquarius habitat and piloting deepwater submersibles. Lad has helped

About the Authors

Photo by Ned DeLoach

develop REEF's marine life education and data collection programs and continues to lead numerous volunteer and research based projects each year. His current focus as REEF's Director of Operations is on addressing the lion-fish invasion including developing and implementing research, outreach, training and control programs throughout the region. To date, Lad has collected, handled and eaten more invasive lionfish from a range of countries than any other person working on the invasion and has helped develop many of the lionfish programs and practices in place throughout the region. This book represents a novel approach to addressing the invasion and is the result of the strong partnerships Lad has helped to align.

David M. Stone

Photo by Wayne Dion

David M. Stone was a professional nature photographer for 35 years, and featured in such publications as Time-Life, National Geographic filmstrips and the principal photographer for the PBS Victory Garden Landscape Guide. In 2008, he retired to the Turks and Caicos Islands, where he volunteers much of his time to preserving and protecting the natural environment of this beautiful country. An active diver, David supports marine conservation and is involved in establishing the non-profit foundation Turks & Caicos Reef Fund to protect and preserve the reefs in the Turks and Caicos Islands.

Resources

Lionfish research and control programs are constantly progressing and yielding new information. For up-to-date information on the lionfish invasion, impacts, removal programs and volunteer opportunities visit the following websites:

- Reef Environmental Education Foundation (REEF) - www.REEF.org/lionfish

- National Oceanic and Atmospheric Administration (NOAA), Center for Coastal Fisheries and Habitat Research - http://www.ccfhr.noaa.gov/stressors/lionfish.aspx

- United States Geological Survey (USGS) Non-indigenous Aquatic Species - http://nas.er.usgs.gov

- On Facebook - REEF Invasive Lionfish Program

The following scientific research papers supplied substantial information and detail in their subject reviews:

Albins, M.A. and M.A. Hixon. 2008. Invasive Indo-Pacific lionfish(Pterois volitans) reduce recruitment of Atlantic coral-reef fishes. Marine Ecology Progress Series 367:233-238.

Fishelson, L. 1975. Ethology and reproduction of pteroid fishes found in the Gulf of Aqaba (Red Sea), especially Dendrochirus brachypterus (Cuvier), (Pteroidae, Teleostei). Pubblicazioni della Stazione zoologica di Napoli 39:635-656.

Fishelson, L. 1997. Experiments and observations on food consumption, growth and starvation in Dendrochirus brachypterus and Pterois volitans (Pteroinae, Scorpaenidae). Environmental Biology of Fishes 50:391–403.

Green, S.J. and I.M. Côté. 2008. Record densities of Indo-Pacific lionfish on Bahamian coral reefs. Coral Reefs DOI 10.1007/s00338-008-0446-8.

Morris, J.A., Jr., and P.E. Whitfield. 2009. Biology, Ecology, Control and Management of the Invasive Indo-Pacific Lionfish: An Updated Integrated Assessment. NOAA Technical Memorandum NOS NCCOS 99. 57 pp.

Morris JA Jr, Akins JL (2009) Feeding ecology of invasive lionfish (Pterois volitans) in the Bahamian archipelago. Environ Biol Fish 86:389–398

Ruiz-Carus, R., R.E. Matheson, D.E. Roberts and P.E. Whitfield. 2006. The western Pacific red lionfish, Pterois volitans (Scorpaenidae), in Florida: Evidence for reproduction and parasitism in the first exotic marine fish established in state waters. Biological Conservation 128:384-390.

Saunders, P.R. and P.B. Taylor. 1959. Venom of the lionfish Pterois volitans. American Journal of Physiology 197:437-440.

Schultz, E. T. 1986. Pterois volitans and Pterois miles: two valid species. Copeia 1986:686–690.

Semmens, B.X., E. Buhle, A. Salomon, and C. Pattengill-Semmens. 2004. A hotspot of non-native marine fishes: evidence for the aquarium trade as an invasion pathway. Marine Ecology Progress Series 266:239–244.

Shiomi, K. M. Hosaka, S. Fujita, H. Yamanaka, and T. Kikuchi. 1989. Venoms from six species of marine fish: lethal and hymolytic activities and their neutralization by commercial stonefish antivenom. Marine Biology 103:285-289.

Vetrano, S.J., J.B. Lebowitz, and S. Marcus. 2002. Lionfish envenomation. Journal of Emergency Medicine 23:379-382.

Whitfield P.E., T. Gardner, S.P. Vives, M.R. Gilligan, W.R. Courtenay, G.C. Ray, and J.A. Hare. 2002. Biological invasion of the Indo-Pacific lionfish Pterois volitans along the Atlantic coast of North America. Marine Ecology Progress Series 235:289-297.

HISTORIC JAMES E. LOCKWOOD REEF HEADQUARTERS
98300 Overseas Highway, Key Largo, FL 33037

Built in 1913, REEF's headquarters building is the oldest structure in Key Largo, Florida. The traditional "Conch-house" architectural style is made of termite-resistant Keys pine, set on concrete piers to resist rotting. Each room was constructed with the rigidity of a sturdy structural cube to resist hurricanes. It was one of the few buildings in the Upper Keys to survive the 1935 Labor Day category 5 hurricane. In 2001, with generous funding from its members and several foundations, REEF purchased the building to serve as its headquarters.

Reef Environmental Education Foundation (REEF)
98300 Overseas Highway, Key Largo, FL 33037
(305) 852-0030 | www.REEF.org